Law 11,340 Maria da Penha

Roberto da Silva Rocha, university professor and
political scientist

Introduction

Human stupidity has no limits.

It always manages to surprise me.

How would it be possible to reduce statistics on
violence against women?

I can't imagine this!

According to data from the Ministry of Justice, the
murders of women reached the incredible and
catastrophic figure of 6.12 women per 100,000
inhabitants in Brazil!

When we consider that in Brazil about 49.9 murders
are committed for each group of one hundred
thousand inhabitants, and that about 37.1 murders of
men are committed for each group of one hundred
thousand inhabitants, you think how absurd the Maria
da law is. Rock!

In Norway, Sweden or Denmark this is the order of
magnitude of murders about 0.5% or 5 per 100,000
inhabitants. We need a Maria da Penha Law in favor
of men's homicides against themselves to get us down

to the index of murdered Brazilian women.... For God's sake, this is mass hysteria and false propaganda... Come out of it, let's be honest , don't fight with numbers!

I call for the condemnation of all men for the continued violations committed against women, mainly establishing for more than 10,000 years such supremacy that it has hegemonically excluded women from any initiative important to humanity. Men created practically everything that exists in modern life without allowing the slightest female participation, as they created, among other
things: Submarine; Steamship Aircraft Vehicles

Computer Operating Systems digitized and analog for computerized devices helicopters propeller Electric generators Electric Welding Ball Pen Washer Hair dryers, semiconductor Microprocessors invented, discovered the
Physics, Chemistry, Mathematics Geography

Philosophy Psychology Medicine Anthropology

Sociology Astronautics Astrology Engineering and finally, left almost nothing for women to discover or invent.

This fact has left women in such a situation that they are unable to prove their intellectual qualities due to the total absence of any opportunity left by males.

That's why people like Maria da Penha suffered aggression for almost a decade (from 1983 to 1993) by her husband and without being able to leave him, she allowed her suffering to continue until he was removed from her side by divorce.

Women need to be supervised, cared for, driven by the male oppression does not allow them to grow and they are unable to break this total dependence male, intellectually, physically, economically and emotionally.

ANNUAL REPORT 2000 REPORT N° 54/01* CASE 12,051 / OEA MARIA DA PENHA MAIA FERNANDES BRASIL 4 April 2001 I. SUMMARY

The UN Human Rights Commission received a demand from Maria da Penha Fernandes, a Brazilian woman, northeastern, married to a naturalized Brazilian born in Colombia named Marco Antônio Heredia, in a scene where the aggression escalated from verbal initially to ways of physical facts there in the state of Ceará where this couple lived.

It could have been another number in the statistics of the many couple fights if it weren't for the fact that the victim had sought Brazilian justice and, dissatisfied with the sentence handed down against her aggressor, sought to sharpen and aggravate the penalty by giving international promotion and publicity to the fact of the aggression using the Forun world's largest rebound after realized their situation where we saw paralyzed due to the fatality of frustrated assassination attempt by part of the aggressor that targeted with a gun shot.

Patient Maria da Penha claims two things:

a) The fifteen-year delay to complete the closure of the defendant's conviction;
b) Violence suffered as a woman.

Any Brazilian who is forced to resort to the Brazilian judicial system suffers from administrative bureaucratic paralysis of the courts and of the legal structure where one can appeal ten times in up to four judicial instances, which extends an action of this type by up to twenty years if the defendant have disposition and resources, taking the delay to the statute of limitations or decay.

Thus, it was not a privilege or persecution over Maria da penha or a lack of interest given her condition as a woman, because the law is blind to the cover of the process, nowhere in the heavy penal code and in the Brazilian penal procedure code is written that the sound of patients the discriminated against on grounds of sex or other status except to highlight some benefit. In this case, Brazilian law is very pro dict in rights more than in duties and obligations always.

The Brazilian Constitution in its fifth article has 134 rights and duties against 34 obligations and restrictions to citizens, creating obligations for the Brazilian State that are difficult and even impossible to fulfill, leaving out only the pleasure and happiness of the citizen as a duty of the State. For now.

So, after punishing Mr. Herédia by the Brazilian justice system within the period and within the measures of criminal dosimetry in accordance with the criminal execution laws, what was the most extravagant thing that Ms. Maria da Penha wanted from the Brazilian jurisdictional system?

The lady from penha wanted revenge on that of the cangaceiros who exterminate the entire family when a member of a northeastern family is murdered by another member of another family and then begins an endless vendetta of revenge with serial killings that will end only when the last member remains of the families involved in this reciprocal revenge killing when the last descendant does not even know the reason or the beginning of so much hatred.

Of course the members of the UN human rights commission known m the culture of hatred of

Northeastern clans of Brazil and known the dilatory mechanisms of the Brazilian legal system with its maximum of injustice and culminated aberration in called severance feature, Brazilian jabuticaba where after once all possible processing of the legal process has been completed.

The irresigned victim still has the power to plead the overthrow of what has been built along the procedural crucis of dozens of years and to pass through the eyes of half a dozen judges in all

instances, still looking for an oversight or a chicanery
to overthrow the judged in a desperate or
very cynical gesture to, through a moment of reverie of
a judge, reverse a fait accompli.

Thus, he sought the maria of the rock roll back the act
of their paralysis in the spine caused by the projectile
gun to u aggressor with extreme measure
and repeat once more condemnation roll back time
and return your unused spine definitely through of the
suffering of all men capable of inflicting suffering on
any woman who crosses the path of an aggressor,
with the power erga omines to turn the suffering
around by applying great suffering or the very serious
threat of great suffering through such great
punishment capable to discourage the likely
aggressor.

The idea is attractive, a punishment so violently
applied in an injunction without going through any of
the slow and time-consuming judicial bureaucratic
instances to discourage the male aggressor regardless
of whatever reasons the woman has given that led the
aggressor to dare to touch a woman by violence The
condition of genetic superiority given by nature
is immanent, which makes the male a murderous
machine against the helpless woman without explicitly
admitting this, given that the woman seen in the law is
on the same level of equality.

Despite the condition given by nature to provide the male twice and half higher bone density than granted by the female genetic, males have a muscular explosion two times largest and macho sexual dimorphism of nature endowed them with a much larger muscle and bone mass.

But the law must blind to all this, and more, ignore the aggression of the woman on and against the male and always act unconditionally in the search for the unconditional protection and defense of the female without ever admitting her inferiority in this or any circumstance. Paradox or contradiction?

So the petition by maria da penha creates extraordinary procedures, not against the delay of the legal instruments established by the normal procedure of the Brazilian justice, given the number of cases in the line of jurisdictional provision and the observation of the constitutional principles that were broken by the law providing special protection for the woman, after the complaint of maria da penha, violated the very principles of constitutional clauses:

a) Due legal process;
b) Broad defense;
c) Right to adversary proceedings;
d) Rejected transit;
e) Presumption of innocence.

If these principles are violated, the very special processes of privileged citizens who have vaginas, whether gender women or not, can be speeded up, as transsexuals declared as functional women for legal purposes.

The commission found maria da penha's complaint admissible in a repetition of the same action already filed in Brazil and judged and handed down, the sentence repeats the condemnation at the request of women's militancy in an exclusively political act within that attitude of political militancy characterized by the new Marxist class struggle in Gramsci's version of the ideological war of position to fragment the social fabric in search of breaking the capitalist liberal society that must be destroyed through new instruments of class struggle strategy.

The only violation of the Brazilian State on maria da penha is the same one that makes a work accident victim wait a year to undergo a medical examination to obtain his benefit, the same one that makes a prenatal exam patient wait a year to undergo a ultrasound, the same way that makes a retiree wait for the federal court to take five to ten years to review the values of a pension, the same that makes an insured seeking retirement by age wait two more years to obtain the beginning of the benefit.

Why in this scenario would there be discrimination on the female gender as the condemnation of the UN human rights commission (in lowercase) made it seem?

So he made it seem that Brazil is a slaughterhouse of women who is exterminating them like flies and that the Brazilian man is a permanent attack on the existence of women in our country!

This evil and perverse man is a very serious threat that has received a maximum degree of attention and violent and exceptional action starting with the actions to implement police stations specially constituted to care for women threatened by this terrible dangerous being called male.

As a general rule, all the media are working in the service of promoting the utmost caution of women against the potential danger to society that the mere existence of men who would be better off if they were banned from the social milieu without any statistics or social research to indicate the least probability of factual proof of these possibilities.

So an open campaign began against the Brazilian male, isolating him and cornering the potential male killer of women in fact.

Nowhere in Maria da Penha's action is Mr. Heredia's voice heard. The Mr. Heredia has never been heard by the Human Rights Commission of the UN.

This Nazi and fascist method is reproduced in women's police stations and in exceptional courts

where the unilateral aggression of the
male pre- convicted ex ante any trial is judged, as
required by the feminist law derived from this process
initiated in the furnace of the theory of secession for
sexual diversity drawn up from the prison writings of
Antônio Gramsci imprisoned in Italy for subversive
activities against the same legally constituted state of
law.

So, Mr. Heredia never exercised in the UN Human
Rights Commission any of the rights awarded to the
complainant Maria da Penha, where it was not even
known what led Mr. Heredia to want to kill his partner.

If he were an unmotivated psychopath, he would be
admitted to an insane asylum, but in this case he was
conscious and in perfect condition to control his
actions and desires.

Neither self-defense nor putative defense was
considered, nor was the reason for the aggression
asked.

Mr. Heredia suffered a trial without qua is both
mitigating and hit all Brazilians males of the anger of a
Northeastern woman in her craving for revenge
without which even weigh the atavistic cultural
background knowledge of any Brazilian sung in versa
and prose in the stigmatization of male
Paraíba muié macho yes sir.

Blind to popular culture northeastern and acts as if no cultural circumstances could provide any sense of seeking understanding the genesis of violence and language of violence ingrained in country music culture e since Cabral de Melo Neto and José de Alencar and others writers including a woman, our Raquel de Queiroz.

But when you want to make a big nonsense nothing happens by improvisation or by accident, the system is and march seeking the destruction of the social contract I implied that freed us from the savagery of the law of retaliation for contractualist society, these Communists never gave up society totalitarian thought and the destruction of freedom.

So not only did it re-judge the case of the aggression against Maria da Penha, but also the UN Human Rights Commission judged the jurisdictional system of the Brazilian State and this resulted in international blackmail forcing Brazil to build a law of exception called the Maria Law of pen number 11340.

Like all victims often become paralyzed inexplicably and irrationally for ten years after its narrative nothing truly suffering aggression without separating the aggressor in a passive attitude almost psychotic pleasure suffering received as if he liked it a masochistic sick atavism and only when a great tragedy happens this process comes to light in society.

It is a pathological clinical case that turns into a criminal case long after a degeneration and loss of control of the addict in applying suffering and the addict in physical and emotional suffering. Both become dependent on each other, victim and aggressor, bypassing all existing physical and moral limits.

After two murder attempts, the slow lady Maria da Penha realized that she could leave her aggressor and live apart from him after all this and for a couple of decades without anyone suspecting this almost pathological leniency in enjoying suffering so much without caring about you herself and her daughter without ever having reported it until she was almost killed while sleeping with the murderer, but is exceptionally active in seeking exceptional help from the UN human rights commission in a turn that is in no way compatible with her extremely passive and tolerant trajectory .

It is a challenge for those who have even half a day of neurons to try to understand how a lady who works outside the home has her profession well formally established, with higher education, well literate cannot defend herself minimally from a persistent aggressor and has never sketched a even a gesture of defense or reprisal, have you never sought police or legal help, perhaps psychiatric help, to avoid the extreme situation, even with two murder attempts against your life?

I've never seen such a flawed and false argument
because it doesn't serve as a plot for a movie or a
novel because it lacks veracity
and logical consistency.

There will never be a movie about Maria da
Penha. The most idiotic and incoherent plot in the
world doesn't deserve a book, but it deserved every
revolution in the folkloric cast of the already ridiculous
Brazilian judicial system.

She has always innocently married a man of whom
she did not know any basic information to place
someone inside her home, according to the account in
her defense, who actually testifies against herself,
showing her confused and careless nature apparently
if not for blind ambition about the possibilities of
marrying a man of far greater possessions than you.

Then the UN human rights commission starts to
exercise the review function of the procedures of the
Brazilian court, abusing its competence and violating
the national autarchic sovereignty
and independence by the HRC.

There is no repair of damage because all human acts
are irreversible, a word that comes out of the mouth
cannot return to the mouth and be undone, nullified,
repaired, a physical aggression cannot be undone
even with punishment and revenge, no penalty returns

or revokes any act nor can it compensate, it is all a fallacy of begging the question of justice.

Not even forewarned by the threat and exemplarity. The only way to punish wrongdoing is to prevent wrongdoing.

All the furor and publicity of Maria da Penha did not remove the suffering or even the wheels of her perpetual chair, this lady lives in the bitterness of her life giving lectures and being exalted and decorated when it is known that nothing will return to her physical and emotional condition from before. It's all useless. Punishment is for nothing. We'll never learn the lesson.

Men still attacked and challenged to be by their counterparts and continue reacting simply because they believe just like the criminal law teaches that vengeance has the power to make the first hurt, and, further, can threaten and prevent the aggressor, but none of that it has worked so far in humanity.

The only thing that changed society was ethics and moral conscience. But that doesn't convince us.

They do not remember that the first violence is the invasion of the other's privacy and the aggressive verbalization of a claim that turns into factual paths

only when the adversary in the dispute touches the
other is that the rule of law and society are moved.

The woman continues to believe that des to spin the
male and instigate and harass in word and gesture
is not the same aggression that perpetrates by violent
physical contact, but the assault began long before
when the male was shredded and his animal instinct
emerges and he reacts in his defense of masculinity
by demonstrating the resumption of his status of
physical superiority, which constitutes the primary
advantage to end any dispute whatsoever, since he
knows that the woman will always lose in the physical
physical arena.

Without wanting to physically submit, he tries to draw a
ration and aggravates the physical aggressions
stimulated by the discourse of false equality of
conditions of the legal protection that he pretends, only
appears after the dispute over the actual routes is
ended by physical defeat.

It is sad to regret the irrational discourse that does not
recognize the weakness and fragility of women, on the
contrary, encourages them, exalting the non-existent
or inefficient equality due to the proportions of the
dispute where help is always late and nothing can be
done.

Let us continue with our irrational discourse, still
reinforced by the stillborn idea of justice as a regulator

of social relations when the contract is of little use
when the client decides to violate the conventions and
there is only a huge amount of work left to appeal for
compensation for the loss without considering at least
time it was already an advantage in favor of the
defendant and the time will never be compensated
and can never be regressed in favor of the plaintiff.

We live deceiving ourselves about the real possibilities
of human justice when we should be concerned with
education for non-violence that prevents and
anticipates potential conflicts. Avoid the first cry, avoid
the first fight, avoid the first lie, avoid the temptation to
take advantage of another person, avoid violating
unauthorized property and privacy, avoid abusing the
other's tolerance and kindness.

No law in the world has prevented or prevented any
crime after being committed based on the calculation
of the cost of risk based on the probability of escaping
punishment or being discovered in the criminal act.

Prevention is confused with threats. Prevention is
teaching and dialoguing to show the advantages of a
decent and egalitarian social contract that does not
blind to differences, producing compensation and
confirming the recognition of the weaknesses and
virtual superiorities immanently granted by nature
itself.

This whole system based on the hatred of the eternal female victim of the male aggressor does not disguise and does not hide the clear truth of the woman's natural physical inferiority, and denying this is already the first step to avoid the solution.

It sounds silly and obvious to say that the woman is surrounded by protection against the male is a crime in itself artificially empowering a
being immanent mind fragile and intending to give guarantees that it will continue to challenge the male to the limit of blows, it is surprising if violence prevention campaigns stopped pretending to attack and nickname the male and asked women to refrain from the risk of aggression, women are not being encouraged to recognize the evident physical superiority of males and instead attack for themselves defend. Only a human being is capable of such madness and irrationality.

Finally, they turned the leniency and delay for the defendant into a malicious perpetration of male in favor of Mr. Heredia when the leniency of justice is against everyone in a sophistic cast of eristic diction riddled with fallacies capable of blushing any
non- feminazi citizen with just a couple of neurons like that machillizing justice and treating it as part of the sexist action against the unprotected woman.

I and all Brazilians wish that justice were agile and minimally rationalized, everyone would be satisfied, but this process of violation of social guarantees in favor of women against men because of a fierce domestic dispute which we do not know who started or who was the culprit as demonstrated in the case file criminal established where the jury deliberated with accompanying of it pari passu and had doubts about the guilt of Mr. Heredia comes to extrajudicial cut unilaterally declare unappealable judgment and the default condemning Mr. Heredia this yes an absurd and unfair fact.

Resigned the party appealed. . Another three years passed until, on May 4, 1995, the Court of Appeal decided on the appeal.

In that decision, it accepted the claim presented extemporaneously and, based on the defense's argument that there were defects in the formulation of questions to the jurors, annulled the Jury's decision.

The UN HRC does not respect the popular sovereignty represented by the popular jury in the legal and appealable judgment within the Brazilian justice system that you used.

Can it be imagined that all Brazilians dissatisfied with judicial decisions thus appealed to international courts for no reason other than their disobedience and stubbornness?

Militants tend to easily accommodate totalitarian ideologies.

An ethnic militant begins by imagining a strong cohesive component capable of coercing forces to face the different.

What happened next was the discovery that the unit is restricted to a single common characteristic.

Altogether they are as diverse as any social group: they have antagonistic football teams; has different cultures musical, theatrical, literary; has a completely diversified leisure option; have different standard of living; has diverse sexuality.

Finally, the only way to guarantee cohesion is to establish a universal totalitarian standard for religion, sexual, musical, cultural, sporting.

The case maria of the rock is only an at the ideological political eschatology known as fighting genres within the international communist hegemony strategy represented by Forun of people who coordinates the famous transnational institution of Forun of Saint Paul.

The Minister of the Federal Supreme Court (STF) Marco Aurélio Mello ordered the return to active service of judge Edilson Rumbelsperger Rodrigues, from the district of Sete Lagoas (MG).

In November last year, he was suspended for at least two years, accused of using discriminatory and prejudiced language in sentences in which he considered the Maria da Penha Law to be unconstitutional.

The magistrate also rejected requests for measures against men who assaulted and threatened their companions.

The decision of the STF minister is preliminary and can be challenged in plenary. Marco Aurélio Mello considered the removal "inappropriate" and stated that the magistrate's statements were made in an "abstract" manner, without referring to a particular person. For him, the judge's sentences are the result of his "individual conception".

"It is possible that one does not agree with the premises of the decision handed down, with a focus on the area of ideas, but this cannot be resolved by distancing the magistrate from the specific attributes of performance, as occurs with availability", stated Marco Aurélio.

In 2007, Rodrigues attacked the law in a few sentences, calling it a "diabolical set of rules". Also according to the judge, the "human disgrace" would have started because of the woman.

"To avenge this set of diabolical rules, the family will be in danger (..) Well, human disgrace began in Eden: because of the woman. We all know, but also because of the naivety, foolishness and emotional fragility of the man", according to excerpts from the judge's decisions.

Rodrigues has responded to administrative proceedings at the CNJ since September 2009. At the time, he denied that there was "excess of language" and defended himself against the accusation of prejudice.

"I didn't offend the party or anyone else. I rebelled against a theoretical law, and even so, part of it. I fight an exaggerated feminism, which neglects the paternal function, which does want equality, but making a point of keeping all the benefits of femininity intact", said the judge.

"Between the excess of language and the posture that seeks to inhibit it, we must stick with the former, as there are adequate means for correction, even if necessary," said the STF minister in his decision. Information is from G1.

Conclusions:

Mrs Maria da Penha

One day, she was lying in her bed when she was suddenly awakened by her husband with a loud bang.

That day the husband, Marcos Heredia, woke up, fed the birds, washed the car, turned on the radio, played the video game, and as he was bored, he took the shotgun and had the id and was going to make some small holes in the back of Maria da penha.

Because of this joke in bad taste, without any motivation, because she was a good lady and an excellent mother and wife, Mr. Marcos was convicted by the popular jury and sentenced to fifteen years in prison.

Dissatisfied with the delay in the trial, Ms. Maria da Penha appealed to the OAS court to denounce the slowness of justice in her case, as the trial took only 10 years, a very rare thing in Brazil, whose justice is known for its speed.

As the due legal process brought against the accused allowed them to be heard by the members of the jury trial, the sentence of fifteen years was reduced to just ten years, to Maria da Penha's displeasure.

Dissatisfied with the outcome, feminists and defenders of women's human rights, victims of typical male violence, managed to enact a law that makes the divorce in fact, in a very simple, summary, unilateral ritual, without the contradictory, without the legitm presumption of innocence of the accused, without due process, allowing the go immediately accused to jail and never can return to your home, being dispossessed of all their belongings and personal effects, professional, emotional, and of value.

Thus, the revenge of women against violent men is achieved, since justice is always insufficient, even seeing her ex-husband condemned by due process, Maria da Penha, now a heroine, will be elevated to the maximum symbol of the defense of justice.

Now, without irony.

You can't cure a man's heartbreak syndrome with his penal confinement. This only sharpens your spirit of revenge, and light a sense of injustice, perhaps, awakens a sense of unevenness of the applied punishment, since the consequences of the Maria da Penha Law determine a fact of divorce that violates conventions and former bridal conventions, hunts down all formal rights of the accused, and acts in an extremely viral, vindictive, exclusionary, irreversible, summary and hasty manner.

Emotional problems should fall within the scope of family psychologists and therapists, not in the hands of a police chief, a bailiff, or GATE, BOPE, GARRA, Civil or Military police officers who have not been trained to understand the diseases of the troubled heart of a wounded love.

The result of these mistakes is that crimes against women have been insignificantly reduced, and time will revoke this great mistake, along with the ill-fated Statute of Children and Adolescents, two tupiniquin jaboticabas idiosyncrasy included in our tangled Brazilian code of legal conduct. Since they lack formal-legal, logical, constitutional arguments, then only statistics will demonstrate the absurdity of this exceptional Law, the true exceptional decree AI-5 of the penal procedure code in a post-dictatorship period in Brazil.

A legal excrescence, the result of the condemnation of the judiciary by the OAS, which condemned the legal process in Brazil, and not Mr. Heredia.

App Driver photographs breasts of customers who are napping in their car and post the photo on the social network.

My notes of repudiation to this idiot who still lives in the romantic age of spying on the female body, at this stage of Brazilian civilization where women, in their majority, vulgarized sexuality in all aspects of moral experience.

Women dying in clandestine clinics, women who spend 15 thousand dollar to have a huge breast, huge ass, clothes packing their body in vacuum, showing all the details of the vagina division, but the idiot still looks at them on the streets, schizophrenics who spend on average 287 dollar a week in aesthetic and jogging training step strength pull push academy strong bodies stores just to not be noticed on the streets and taxis, and urban transport, in malls, in apps, when will men understand this feminine logic?

Who has the lowest IQ? The male who succumbs to feminine erotic and infantile artifices, or the flamboyant woman wanton with an air of innocent and naive?

Schizophrenia and psychopathy female fic plow for many decades set in only the names of hurricanes until changed the practice under the politically correct protests.

The social practice of common sense does not always defy logic and allows all women to perform healthy and excusable madness twice a month for ten days under the pretext of menstrual cramps.

Imagine if the males had this design socially permitted and rich so once a year they had a day to blow up hatred against everything and against all because of a colic or other pain or other discomfort to your moody. This is equality.

Militants tend to easily accommodate totalitarian ideologies.

An ethnic militant begins by imagining a strong cohesive component capable of coercing forces to face the different.

What happened next was the discovery that the unit is restricted to a single common characteristic.

Altogether they are as diverse as any social group: they have antagonistic football teams; has different cultures musical, theatrical, literary; has a completely diversified leisure option; have different standard of living; has diverse sexuality.

Anyway, only way to ensure cohesion is to establish a universal standard for totalitarian religion, sexual, musical, cultural, sports way.

The Soviet and Chinese communism do extraordinary things that no capitalism or could get, because of certain political parameters inexorably inherent and exclusive system that can not be played on plebiscitary liberal capitalism.

The doctrinal error of communism was its intellectual and doctrinal arrogance, which claimed to be totalitarianism that does not exclude anything from people's lives from its intellectual tutelage.

Thus, abolish morality, religion, culture, science, state, family, and substituted them for their unprecedented pattern.

Arrogance defeated communism.

There is no nation without heroes;

There is no science without an answer for everything;

There is no religion without miracles;

There is no philosophy without ambiguous abstractions;

There is no civilization without tradition;

There is no culture without myths;

There is no history without an epic.

There is no ideology without self-righteousness.

It all started with sinners.

There victims of sin needing the salvation of the lost soul.

Then came the slave needing release.

Then came the people oppressed by slavery who were freed from cruel captivity.

So it was the despised and stoned harlots who were forgiven of their sins for not throwing the first stone.

The downtrodden increased the list.

Lepers were no longer segregated nor were the Gentiles.

Women were despised, forming a huge minority with foreigners and the poor from ancient Egypt to the Greece of learned philosophers . .

Then there were the servants, and the poor, and the orphans, the elderly, the chronically ill, the little children, the blacks, the homosexuals, the homeless, the excluded, the politically persecuted, the northeastern, the illiterate, then society noticed that the list of the persecuted and the needy was endless.

What did you do to solve so much need?

She invented the ideology of gender, feminism, sexism, communism, the excluded, politically correct, egalitarianism, assembly, all kinds of victimism and populism, caudilloism, protectionism, poor people obsessed with the idea of guilt and punishment, came to Islamophobia, Zionism, Fascism, Nazism, Castroism, Nationalism, Bolivarianism, Lulisno, Varguism, Human Rights, Anti- war, Environmentalism, Ecologism, Veganism, Christianity, Buddhism and all forms of intellectual and moral autism, and discriminatory forms of compensatory privileges.

The teaching of history has its serious limitations that I was aware of from my childhood.

The current geography education has been hijacked by the two worst types of political militants who never rely on scientific knowledge to be able to trumpet Marxist catastrophes to blackmail the population and politicians with their predictions that are actually just prophecies of chaos and far-fetched catastrophes.

As predictable as an earthquake, floods, tsunami and volcanic explosions.

History is only a fraction of the facts whose registration criterion is their relevance to posterity.

The problem for historians and historiography is to highlight what is relevant to whom, for what and why.

Historical facts and acts are narrated in the news non-stop, and the controversy surrounding this makes us believe that with all the capacity to generate discussion, the facts are still only agreed and consensus versions of the multiple and underlying reality and therefore always subject to the diversity of readings according to the teleology and tautology mind of the hegemonic intellectual class.

We will never know the real facts of September 11, 2001; we'll never know about the 2014 World Cup for the blackout of the Brazilian team; we will never know the fall of Saddam Hussein and Kadaffi.

These are just post-truth versions.

Geography immersed in communist messages and catechizing about an unequal and unjust world, where everything is unfairly distributed, where a single country has a third of the world oil reserves, another has ninety percent of the world rare earths or niobium, another is rich too much economically and another just misery like that in this right little world, the Himalayas would not exist because it is too high, inaccessible for poor Ghanaian children to play and the Sahara without water to plant rice.

How horrible! But, the psychopaths of egalitarianism!

Ideologies that want to level the entire universe will never understand that to have a habitable planet they need a star that looks like hell! Right in heaven!

Lawyers know that the only possible story in a criminal record is one that is limited to the letters and words that are recorded on paper, any inference outside the records does not belong to the legal world and sphere. Therefore, the sentence of the record and the only truth is the one that belongs to the legal world. Nothing can overflow from the facts reported there, nothing absolutely nothing. The only possible story of a crime.

The pedagogy of punishment

in Brazil is implementing the current Anti pedagogy: a Pedagogy of punishment.

It is a new-old current that advocates the Pavlovian punitive correction.

Instead of teaching, supporting institutions that instruct and provide social training to individuals, she believes that punishment is more effective than educating and sharing social values rather than reinforcing social institutions shared and shared by society.

Thus, they intend to replace family, church, moral norms, and traditional customs with legal rules that adopt draconian punishments as severe as offenses against social minorities.

Minorities would be the targets to be contemplated by the expectation of protection offered by the new pain pedagogy.

Thus, the homophobic aggressor, the male aggressor, the journalist aggressor, the pedophile aggressor, the driver aggressor, the antisocial aggressor of all kinds are punished. Briefly.

Punishment was chosen instead of social reinforcement to frame antisocial behavior because in authoritarian minds there is only an alternative to the imposition of their will and standardized behavior as the only alternative to frame the different, the divergent and the excluding in the expectations of a monolithic society, undifferentiated, from the single standardized hegemonic thought.

Any and all deviant behavior is perceived as a serious social threat, as a chronic disease and unspeakable, intolerable, unacceptable, so it should be eliminated the without giving chance for recovery, treatment, rehabilitation. Punishment alone is sufficient for these cases.

The expectations of this current are of a world without social changes, without conflicts, without differences, without tolerance.

They are authoritarian and self-sufficient in their absolute wisdom, they cannot relativize or share social values in their mental and intellectual confinement.

They believe themselves to be bearers of the unique truth. Nor do they even consider alternative solutions for society.

These heralds of truth spread their gospel of the perfect utopian idea of a perfect society without any doubt that they are doing their best, so they believe that people who disagree with them just ignore the truth, and don't know what's best for they, therefore, need to protect the entire ignorant and misinformed, manipulated and alienated society.

We do not know how they discovered these truths they believe in, but we do know that they have no self-censorship, alter- censorship, nor self-criticism or alter- criticism. Such is the certainty of their convictions, irrefutable, so certain that they do not seek to justify them, as they are self-evident truths, so clear and so dear to these heralds of the new -perfect- world.

They believe that if they didn't exist the world would already be sunk in the most complete chaos. Its mission to redeem the world is justified from any failure, or unorthodox act, even extralegal and unethical acts, of course, within its restricted and closed ethics.

In their revolutionary, revisionist and society renovating trajectory, they need to act quickly and without the caution of other times, as they are the prophets and guides of humanity, because people who have not yet understood their noble mission will one day do so, in the future, justified by the legitimation of beneficial results.

Certainly, that will come to all citizens and to society, which, thus grateful, would be rewarded for the present sacrifice and for the misunderstandings of the present moment of false abstinence of reason. We are in the times of an old religion called one-thought where divergence and plurality are prohibited.

This moment requires a cool head and data analysis to draw the line between despair and despondency; of wisdom and assertiveness.

Amazingly, the problem is well located.

And it is long and difficult to understand.

Come on, in stages.

Sociology creator Émile Durkheim became famous for studying suicide.

He was surprised to find the origins of the selfish suicide because there were two other types of suicide: anomic and social suicide or altruism.

He first discovered that the Protestant religion has the highest number of suicides.

Amazing!

So he went looking for the reason.

 Criminal social surveys showing things that always surprise us.

We don't like this data.

Much less of the causes.

Most of the homicides of married people are carried out by the other spouse.

Most rapes are caused by relatives and friends.

Blacks are the majority of the murdered.

But, black people are the majority of murderers.

How crime is seen is structurally equated; we know who practices and why.

The solution and the way forward are the problems.

It moves against social and moral expectations.

Is home hell on earth? The most dangerous place to live? Are domestic tensions inevitable? Does the informality of domestic life loosen and relativize the spaces of privacy?

It's not the right time to let go.

Civilization is crumbling.

Our enemies almost defeated us.

They are the enemies of our civilization's tradition.

Communism has been cornered, but it resists alive like a virus attenuated, sheltered, withdrawn, hibernating awaiting its best chance, which undoubtedly are the moments of crisis of financial hardship to delude the crowds with the false magical and desperate exit.

Communism is a sordid enslavement of a political elite
over the entire population, totalitarian and ruthless.

The second threat is cocaine, and its equivalents,
crack, heroin and ecstasy and their respective
equivalents.

Along with alcohol, they provide the anesthetic for
daily hardships.

The problem with illicit drugs and legal drugs
is addiction .

They are addictive and produce dependence and
moral and physical decay. Were it not for that, it would
be paradise in the promised land.

Then comes the third modern plague which is the
self- extinction of our deliberately executed human
species.

People are not reproducing.

And the worst: they are committing suicide.

Countries have abolished marriage, replaced by
casual unions, and homosexual couples, legally called
homo-affective before being constitutional, by an

incidental decision of the STF judges, without respecting the house that makes the country's laws.

Thus, we must unite our forces over all Christian doctrinal differences for the salvation of humanity that still remains .

Separating men from women in the war of discourse on violence against women, conveniently fits the pretense of preserving the human species by reducing population according to some to half a million people who would live comfortably on earth only the rich, according to the proposals of
the illuminating globalists .

We live in a new scenario of an as-yet-dominant type of war.

The kind of subliminal warfare.

This new weapon of war was carefully created by a communist thinker named Gramsci.

It's that tactic of repeating the seemingly illogical argument.

Because of the stupefaction caused by the reduction to the absurd, it produces the shock of psychic violation, reducing mental and psychological defenses through the effect of paralysis in the face of the paradigmatic paradox.

So, the sophists use paralogy to lead their arguments through a sophistical cast, provoking the contradiction by redaction.

This war of words uses the diction of the scream without caring about the arguments. Until exhausting the interlocutor.

Then, the incorporation of the adversary's own contrary arguments passes to repetitions of his eristic verbosity, now without resistance and without the anesthetized intellectual block.

Doublethink:

the housework is so useless, as feminists, that the woman only works even true when you have a job outside the home, those who work at home is sub citizen, housewife, domestic, but .....

when it's time to retire, then no, housework of the humiliated and disqualified housewife, underutilized and without the dignity of work outside the home counts for a lot, according to the same feminists this unimportant work becomes work like any other outside the home. home, real work, so much so that women with double shifts continue to die long after the male, proving that working at home is very painful, contradicting the rhetoric of the same feminists who insist on saying that women only work if they are outside work. From home.

Understand.

What about femicide? (women murder)

Feminist logic says that this is murder just for being a woman.

Understand.

The woman is killed regardless of being a woman.

Unaware of any other situation or circumstance, whether male self defense, assault, disputes materials, religious disputes, nothing, but nothing matters, the woman is dead because men just hate the women and want to exterminate them, is such a silly argument, who say that femicide is a simple act of assaulting a woman as a human being fragile at a disadvantage would be an offense to women and Logic to feminazista not allow any physical inferiority inherent to women, except in MMA, WWF, UFC, in the Olympics where women are only physically equal to men only in riding, archery and target shooting.

Dog world, full of contradictions and a lot of politically correct stupidity.

The Greatest Intellectual Fraud of the 20th Century

What would be the greatest intellectual fraud of the 20th century?

How can an entire civilization be defrauded of a concept without factual proof in the test of History, Sociology, Anthropology and Geography, without fear of trampling on statistical methods and all investigative methodology?

Could it be thought that this was a religious fraud?

How could one build a reinterpretation of the History of humanity with such a universal, absolute, generic, deterministic concept as for example insinuating and imagining that it would simultaneously happen all over the world, in every geographical and temporal place, the same cruel phenomenon as it were, for example, a phenomenon of a single universal language spoken throughout the history of mankind, in all points of the earth's geography, in all cultures of the world and at the same time became for thousands of years a naturally permanent phenomenon?

It would be possible that this fact occurred in humanity during more than fifty thousand years of civilization and pre- civilization and that only in the century. XX was perceived such a phenomenon?

According to the theory of violation and psychic containment of the collective unconscious, there is no possible way out of the prison of collective consciousness.

This phenomenon is observed when, for example, inside a prison of historical consciousness, it is not possible for a human being to see another possibility of escaping from the feudal system, since it never existed and will not exist another alternative to the feudal system, whether for the serf or for you, whether for the vassal or for the noble or for the clergy, once born within this system that lasted 987 years, no chance would have a human being to change or flee from his eternal destiny while living within the social network. During the Middle Ages everything that human beings should know was informed to them by an intercessor of the clergy.

Obey without questioning, listening without meditating, living without a purpose other than serving God and his Lord, submitting to clerical and noble feudal orders.

It was to fulfill all obligations, to marry whoever was determined to them, to live without reason and to die for the deterministic social order.

How many who would challenge that social order from within it would not survive even for the historical record, internal struggles were waged to fill vacancies in lifetime positions that were created by the death or death of its post-donor occupants, or by fraud, or by murder between nobles and clerics, this was how the feudal order was reproduced.

In the feudal order only a small group of bureaucratic intellectuals and priests were endowed with the privilege of examining the scrolls and thus passed the secrets of writing and reading to their heirs, one only chosen to be the apprentice of the secrets of the scrolls, certainly one in twenty thousand, fifty thousand, or one hundred thousand individuals could read and write.

Scrolls were handwritten and copied by anyone who could pay sky-high sums for authentic copies, so ancient and medieval literature survived until the early Renaissance when Gutemberg created the first mechanized publishing press in Europe, popularizing books for the West.

The medieval world was a world closed in feuds, with no circulation of currency, no circulation of goods, no circulation of products, no circulation of people, no circulation of ideas, no circulation of news, so nothing changed in that world.

How could anyone produce behavior other than what
their limited world expected?

How could a Muslim boy think differently from the
unique expectations presented to him from his small
and contingent world?

Outside his belief system this little Muslim has no
social references, no family, no other beliefs, no
friends, no roots and would be a stranger outside his
Muslim world.

It was a world without nights, where at the end of
daylight nothing more happened until the sun came
back to light.

It was a world where news did not circulate on radio
networks, newspapers, television, internet, fax, only
letters for those who could read, where news was
announced live in squares, as there were no sound
amplifiers or loudspeakers, neither phone nor
smartphones, nor social networks such
as facebook or whatsapp, as communication was
difficult in those times of transport to rowing and sailing
ships, and horse carriages.

Thus, without contextualizing and without qualifying
the ancient times and the difficulties in the circulation
of ideas and information, a world where public school
was only invented by the Greeks only five hundred

years before Christ for only 5% to 10% of the citizens who were a category that excluded women, slaves, foreigners and the dispossessed.

So in that blind, deaf and mute world, where the privileged were the noble, clerical and illiterate landlord elites like the rest, to speak of gender discrimination alone is an intellectual extravagance, where slavery and servitude only disappeared from humanity when the human productive force was surpassed by the steam and electric machines of the Industrial Revolution of the second half of the 19th century in England, then Germany and finally the rest of Europe, but even so the Industrial Revolution created the servitude of the industrial proletariat that only had the labor rights recognized with Socialism and revolutionary Marxism.

Karl Marx devoted his entire life to examining the inequality and social injustice of workers and peasants in RI, but neither he (no other scholars, male or female) discovered or questioned any gender inequality in society: the proletarians, the proletarians, male and female workers in industrial centers who transformed degraded labor into industrial inputs that from the army of idle labor extracted the added value of degraded labor, including and mainly exploiting child and youth labor, mercilessly, in the worst conditions that he ever dreamed of a feudal lord or that he imagined a slave master.

You worked without interruption until exhaustion, or until someone got sick, died, or gave up.

Such was the human side of the Industrial Revolution in Liverpool or any European industrial city.

The fraud

From where we could see the gender privileges that feminazists accuse the masculine side of humanity of having denied them space in the so-called sexist world, if not because of the very inappetence of the gender woman in disputing a miserable space in the slums of the Liverpool factories, otherwise the more restricted ability to work 20 hours straight, which was the only requirement to dispute a place in the struggle of the city or country worker, if she could sell another product more valuable than her labor?

Its beauty, as it always did. Were it not for the testimony of Taj Mahal, and other vehement testimonies and unforgettable cases in history, almost this piece of fiction about the unimportance of women who gained an unusual and inexplicable reverberation, unusual about what is falsely seen as the devaluation of the feminine in the History of humanity that almost destroyed the relationship between people, regardless of politically correct gender.

Taj Mahal witnesses the passion of an Indian nobleman for a woman, the love so great that he immortalized his beloved in the mausoleum regarded as one of the eight wonders of world architecture. Built between 1630 and 1652 in Agra, India just to show the immense love of Maharaja Shahdjaham to a single woman in his life who loved more than himself.

His favorite honored wife was named Aryumand Banu Begam, whom he affectionately called Mumtaz Mahal.

Another obvious case of unfathomable love sparked the Trojan War, but it is more part of Greek mythology than history.

It occurred between 1200 BC and 1300 BC.

Princess Helen had been kidnapped by Troy's enemies the Achaeans.

It so happened that while visiting Sparta, Paris, son of King Priam of Troy, falling in love with Helen, decided to kidnap her, so more than a thousand ships were sent to rescue her.

Other historical love affairs were the odysseys of Nefertiti and Cleopatra. Cleopatra seduced a Roman emperor, and at the same time the Egyptian Pharaoh, year 50 BC. Mark Antony the Roman and Ptolemy XIII the Egyptian Pharaoh.

Before entering into considerations about intergender relationships, it is good to remember that he only had access to a good wife who could pay with dowries that varied according to the beauty of the lady to be won.

This habit, still very common in Africa, can leave many men single because they do not have material goods to marry their loved ones, goods that can range from a few cattle to thousands of head of cattle, and thousands of hectares of land.

Where was that Nazi speech that women have always been a sexual object despised and despised without importance in the male world, if men were never exchanged or wanted as consorts in exchange for goods to be coveted, this privilege always fell to the beauty represented by the ideal feminine?

Only the value available to the worker, which was his debased labor, was bought for an hour of feverish work, the only merchandise available to the despoiled worker was sold. According to Marxist language, the proletarian was exploited for the added value of the only input that interests the industrial capitalist or rural capitalist: their time.

It was at this time that, once again, the male workforce proved to be more productive that the social system started to value more and pay more for that workforce in terms of productivity, with fewer interruptions, greater strength and more work capacity, it was It is natural that children and women were less in demand in the labor market.

It happened recently in Communist China where the restriction of one child per couple naturally determined that parents wanted a boy instead of a girl, as this represented a greater guarantee of security for their own parents' old age.

Without this ideological gender discourse, society over the centuries accommodated the social roles of gender according to the socioeconomic determinations that historically and naturally in every corner determined a double role for the female sex in the working world, neither inferior nor superior, only roles: the man sold only his labor; the woman could compete by making the trade off between her labor, or, something of greater value than labor: her beauty.

For the highest value, female beauty has left its female workforce in the background in the utilities market.

Just a matter of cost-benefit and opportunity cost, a product with an inelastic offer with no substitute and no replacement.

The feminine beauty. Once again, the technology of the third industrial revolution came to rescue female

labor, where the tertiary sector isolated male factors
such as strength and physical resistance as
determining factors of productivity in the labor market.

Telematics, computers, organization, management
information systems and financial services dominated
the main economic activities, leaving to the secondary
and primary sectors of the economy, with the
exception of the oil sector, the primacy of the
locomotive of modern States.

So, after two and a half century and a half of trade off
between the offer of female beauty and the offer of
female labor, the discourse became fiercer around the
issue of gender, then came the great intellectual fraud,
which is to transform a natural choice of labor market
in a false ideological question, as if a gender
conspiracy by simple prejudice, called chauvinism,
wanted to exclude women from the productive society
for the simple desire of male conspirators.

Thus, the greatest intellectual fraud has been built
that, if not stopped in the present time, will
be irreparably built in a historical review in an honest
intellectual future, when the moment of initial shock of
that moment of confusion and dissimulation and
victimism, the greatest of all forgeries, has passed.
historical intellectuals of humanity in the twenty-first
century will be recognized as: feminism,
or feminazism.

Before the third wave of revolution, male labor competed with no competitors to match, but not now: for the first time in the history of civilization, there is no gender advantage.

This empties the feminist discourse of gender ideology, since the demonstration effect of male, western and white labor dominated in science, arts and sports with its total hegemony, and not just of male gender: their ethnic superiority to the inhabitants of the high cold latitudes.

With the capitalism of the third wave of the industrial revolution, which corresponds to robotized, programmed machines, computers, the economic system centered on the tertiary sector, services gained prominence in the economy resulting in greater migration from the countryside to the cities, with the emptying of the countryside, with the displacement of gross labor to offices, stores, banks, commerce, the financial sector, the health sector, the education sector, the leisure and entertainment sector, for the arts and mass culture, cinema, theater, industrial productions of books, music, magazines, newspapers, fashion, the service sector in the history of humanity has never been so hegemonic with the mass media such as television, the internet, completely suffocating the primary and secondary sectors, except for a few niches such as the oil sector and the extraction of precious stones, and gold.

The third wave buried the labor-intensive industrial sector by replacing human labor with robots, and the mechanization of agriculture mowed down work in the fields.

At this time, legal rules were created preventing women from being soldiers, from attending schools, from studying, from becoming autonomous, which was a strategic mistake, but it only enshrined the customs of more than five millennia where gender roles seemed to be accommodated by human culture, without dispute, of women openly, which shows that: either the woman was indolent, or the woman was fully satisfied with the social division of social work.

Exceptions were: the Greek women of the island of Lesbos; matriarchal tribes on several continents; the warrior amazons; Joana D'arc; European Queens Antonietas in Portugal, Queen Isabela of Spain; Queen Elizabeth in Great Britain; princesses, Queen Victoria in England; Female pharaohs like Nefertiti and Cleopatra of ancient Egypt. No statute prevented these women from doing what they did or what they were. It wasn't a privilege.

The male carried humanity on his back in the worst moments of the preservation of the human species ensuring its survival and prosperity. Thus, the woman awakened to the labor market, but found it dominated by males, at this time the womem lib was born, a movement for equality in the labor market only in the tertiary sector, services, since there was never a feminist demand for occupying jobs in the heavy, primary and secondary sectors.

Even today there is a noisy absence of women's demand for these jobs not only in the primary and secondary sectors, but also in the more arid areas of the tertiary sector from feminist demands in engineering, in the arduous competitions of sports such as mixed boxing (man versus woman), mixed wrestling, motocross, motorcycle speed, high performance single-seater racing such as Formula One, Indy Car, and both when looking for high areas risk and great physical energy.

Because?

In the high latitudes of cold countries, the geographical conditions were created for the main winners awarded in Nobels in all categories to emerge, and they do not exclude genders only, geographical exclusion of the inhabitants of the tropics and the equator, indicating a geographical determinism.

The simplification and reductionism to the gender factor was the biggest of all the feminists' ideological mistakes because it finds no support in history other than anger and resentment in not being able to explain their indolence and accommodation to the trade off factors of offers of amenities in having to offer between two competing products: their workforce or their

feminine beauty, women in their majority would not
have the option of beauty.

Because beauty has a value far above the value of the
labor it could offer, this in itself establishes a trade off
that tends to be unbalanced and radical, which is
why women are unhappy about not having the
physical beauty factor or not being willing to offer the
their physical beauty in the commodity market derived
their victimism in relation to the painful history of males
who fought since cave times for the survival of the
species of homo sapiens, hard fighting with swords,
spears, bow and arrow, toiling with axe,
sledgehammer and with their callused and sore hands,
and yet without gaining the recognition of such
righteous feminists.

***physical beauty meaning:

a) physical attraction,
b) well-balanced face,
c) slim body,
d) attractive,
e) good health,
f) well-groomed hair,
g) good reputation,
h) youth,
i) well-groomed skin,
j) good presentation,
k) social etiquette,
l) sympathy,
m) discretion,

n) delicacy,
o) docility.

Morality

What is moral?

Moral is a behavior (action, or abstention) consciously
adopted before established objective rules.

Such moral behavior is nothing more than a diverse
and personal interpretation, of an intrinsically
subjective and conscious nature, which modifies the
norms according to personal convenience in a different
way from the objective norms.

Since Plato's Myth of the Cave (Aristocles) it was
clear that the world is a concept created by each
individual, given that each person's perception of
reality depends on their ability to understand and their
perception of reality.

So reality is unique for a given individual.

There is no concrete, real object, except as a
representation of the objective fact in the subjective
process of recognizing the world.

Schopenhauer in his famous book The World as Will
of Representation, Kierkgaard ,

Husserl, Hidegger these all termed phenomenologists, including Plato and Kant, controversially expressed phenomenologically, that is, subjectively, from what they disagree with each other within the limits of interpretation and reinterpretation subjective, of what it represents to itself of reality and Phenomenology, a term only revealed by Husserl.

Thus, the concept of morality can only be understood as the subject's internalization of behavioral expectations in society, that is: his individualistic and selfish utilitarian vision on which his personal decision-making system is based.

To avoid this liberality of interpretations about what each individual should decide on what is best for themselves without considering the consequences outside their personal scope and which could go against their private interests, so that everyone has the same rights and utilities ensured together, so that the collective gains at the expense of sacrificing the prerogatives of each one in particular, the output called Ethics emerges, which is the collective and mandatory practice that imposes on each individual in particular the loss of part of their privileges and the suppression of any prerogative or the loss of part of their rights so that the sum of all individual utilities does not result in collective harm.

As each individual per se would be incapable of making this calculation of collective utility based on

their particular view of what would be an advantage
only for themselves, the rules of Ethics need to be
adhered to despite the individual calculation that each
would make in view of the sacrifice they would have to
make for the good that is indirectly shared with them in
the collective.

This utility calculation does not allow a selfish
individual to clearly recognize the advantages for the
collective, so the rules of ethics are imposing and
generally impose some disadvantage at the entrance
(means) that turns into an advantage at the exit
(ends).

In Ethics, means justify ends.

Nothing can be good if ethically unacceptable means
are used.

I wonder how Catholic and Protestant Christians felt
about the reality of eighteenth-century slavery.

They were families of white Europeans, praying and
doing their penances and ritual ordinances on
a Sunday, there contrite, praying and praying, even
though at that same moment the same humanity and
the right to worship were denied to their slaves nearby
in the slave quarters, in the warehouses of slaves,
they were denied the dignity of dressing, eating at the
table, having a family, loving each other, marrying,

having affection, having feelings, they were bodies
without the right to their religions, to marry, they were
now goods, now barter goods, sold and bought like
horses, were examined naked like any work animals.

So is ethics a circumstantiality, which depends on
temporal and geographic social convention?

Are there no absolute values for ethics?

Of course there are absolute values, and these
absolute values, which have been violated, are: the
right to life, private property, right to autonomy, right to
choose and right to personal inviolability.

Such rights have always existed since the sapiens left
the cave and began life together, in groups, in
communities, in clans, in society, such inalienable and
non-negotiable rights have always existed since then.

Occasionally social schemes try to relax those rights
for the use of coercive force, through domination of
wars on other groups when you impose submission
that it starts by slavery, sexual servitude and the
exclusive taxation of peoples and nations defeated in
clashes and achievements of spoils of war and
conquest.

Slavery and servitude were not innocent acts nor were they contingent acts, they were unnatural and premeditated acts under any circumstances, because they were not universal, they excluded relatives, the most beloved members of clans, families, the elite, they were punishments imposed on enemies and to disliked foreigners.

The Roman Catholic Church did not possess them, but it did not take up the condemnation of black slavery.

Tacit confession of awareness of the evil and discrimination caused by the slave system. Not everything that is accepted and endorsed by society can be accepted as ethical and morally correct.

The inviolable principles are: physical integrity, mental integrity, psychic integrity, sexual integrity, emotional integrity, self-image integrity, integrity of beliefs, cultural integrity, ethnic integrity, integrity of choice, parental integrity, the integrity of material property, the integrity of intellectual property, the integrity of artistic-cultural property, the integrity of the home, the integrity of the use of time, the integrity of the work activity, the integrity of the professional activity and the intellectual integrity.

This is a case of immoral law because the ends do not justify the means, and the processes of the Maria da Penha law are extremely immoral for violating the principle of equal treatment and other paragraphs of

Article 5 of the CF88 and constitutional amendments. Nothing justifies correcting and making a greater mistake than the offense you want to repair.

The West , in its enlightened intolerance against other cultures, pretends to digest them without accepting them, pretends to understand without accepting it, as the Jesuits did with the natives of the South American and Central continents.

Now ask the Vatican if the missions of evangelization were civilizing fact, or making the mea guilt admit that the Vatican vilified and abused the forestry in their status of social, religious and cultural?

How much longer will it take for the intolerant to realize their intolerance towards the other civilization that affronts their civilizing principles?

We witness here or anywhere in the world, with decimal exceptions, the intolerance of homo-affectives against the intolerance of homophobics, both accusing each other of intolerance.

Each consciously violates each other's religious, ethical and moral principles to ensure the reason that the other is acculturated, outdated and uncivilized, both social behaviors are as old as prostitution, being from time to time execrated and tolerated, in cycles stories that span the Middle Ages, the Renaissance, the Ancient Ages, and the Modern and Contemporary Ages.

Mutatis mutantis, nothing is perpetual because social values will never be absolute values, just like the models of State and government, they are neither absolute nor perpetual:

a) freedom,
b) democracy,
c) tyranny,
d) capitalism

everything passes, everything becomes a thousand facets in combined and mixed models of

a) Christian democracy,
b) liberal democracy,
c) parliamentary democracy,
d) direct democracy,
e) indirect democracy,
f) republican liberalism,
g) social liberalism,
h) monarchical parliamentary liberalism,
i) monarchical presidentialism,
j) parliamentary presidentialism,
k) tyrannical presidentialism,
l) presidentialism for life,
m) democratic presidentialism.

Thus variants of truth teach us that the absolute values exist only in the minds of radical fundamentalists of the right, the left, the monetarists radical capitalist, neoliberal liberalist, the globalism extreme "isms",

Protestants as fundamentalist as the extreme Islamists in indicating that the truth can be right in the middle or more to the right or more to the left. We will never know that.

*"**The** beginning of society : marked as a 'first revolution', the construction of shelters and the constitution of families determined the end of nomadism. The language takes on tribal characteristics and this was a time of relative happiness, with the appearance of love. The arising evils will be vanity and comparison."* Jean Jacques Rousseau – Discourse on the origins and foundations of inequalities in human society...

Economics theorists have built an interesting anthropological hypothesis about the origin of agriculture, the rearing of domestic animals and the captive breeding of small domestic animals for food supply.

This theory says that about 50,000 years ago it was the female homo sapiens who invented the domestic economy, agriculture, the spoken language, the raising of domestic animals, created the house, created the first domestic furniture.

The male homo sapiens at this time did not participate in domestic life, which was formed by the group of women, children and human babies. We know this for certain because only in the last five thousand years has human culture begun to establish the association between heterosexual sex and reproduction.

So the male sapiens completely ignored the family life as we know it today, formed by a heterosexual couple as a breeder of the human species.

This fact is the foundation of the history of human culture.

In her historic solitude, wandering through the wild, spending about nine months pregnant and having to take care of her offspring during the puerperium periods, the female sapiens only took care of her partners, as the male thought it had nothing to do. With that awkward situation in which adult human females sexually every nine months were involved.

After the postpartum period, the human baby's lactation time was long. Alone.

The sex for male homo sapiens was indistinct: men, women, old, young, sisters, aunts, mothers, grandmothers, nothing escaped because the foundations of family ties had not been established, because male sapiens lived hunting, traveling, nomad, and collecting food of fortune, in groups of male sapiens males, sometimes returning to the circle where he had been casually born.

How to fix the male close to the females and segregate him from the group of males, making him sedentary?

This was the challenge of female sapiens.

So, female sapiens could not constantly accompany male sapiens on their journeys of hunting and gathering food of fortune, because they were always pregnant, nursing or carrying their offspring, their household items, without knowing who the parents of their offspring were, - if they could associate the sexual act with the act of pregnancy - the females cleverly created some behavioral tactics that together became a very efficient strategy to solve this problem:

a) They invented the concept of feminine beauty;

b) Invented the family;

c) Invented love;

d) Invented male-female sexuality;

e) Invented marriage;

f) They invented fidelity;

g) Invented the home;

h) Invented agriculture;

i) Invented the creation of domestic animals;

j) Invented the Economy;

k) invented private property;

l) They invented savings;

m) They invented the rules of morals and ethics;

n) Invented religion;

o) Invented human culture;

p) They invented chauvinism, then feminism

Thus, they created attractions for the sapiens males to be interested in staying close to the sapiens females and the offspring of the sapiens females without knowing that they had a genetic participation in that reproduction process, a priori, therefore, the females had to create many interesting attractions for the males exchanged his freedom as a nomadic animal for sedentarization with offspring that he would not assume as part of his genetic quota.

What female ingenuity!

The concept of beauty is a female invention, according to the philosopher Rousseau, when the human female created it in prehistory to distinguish itself from other females to catch and attract the attention of the male of the homo species.

It turns out that the prehistoric male was nomadic and promiscuous. For the male, every woman was equal, without distinction, any one would do, except for an eventual illness or old age.

At that time the co-relation of cause and deed between sex, the male, pregnancy and reproduction had not yet been established in culture and biology science yet.

It happened that females, also promiscuous and unfaithful like males, went through three occasions in their lives when they needed the companion presence they were at the end of pregnancy, childbirth, and in the suckling phase of the offspring, when they needed to be helped in the childbirth and in the postpartum phase to carry out their activities.

So the female needed to invent the family, and consequently moral love, while the male only knew physical, sexual, casual love.

So the female invented beauty, starting to dress up to attract the male and make him sedentary, to make the sex a commodity, so he would always remember that female, show that she was different from other females, beautiful, wearing adornments, taking care of her hair, drawing attention to parts of the body and for his identity which was mainly his face, thus starting a competition with other females for the male's attention.

Females began to check the things that most attracted males in their bodies to highlight them, and to hide the parts considered less attractive, to create emotional and moral bonds.

Thus was the concept of beauty invented.

What engineering!

The woman invented the family, moral love, beauty, monogamy, jealousy, to maintain
the exclusivity and fidelity of the male through affection.

The woman, to escape the effort of hunting, domesticated the animals that served as food; to escape the collection of food, he buried and transplanted some vegetables and realized that they could live and grow, thus inventing agriculture and saving walks around the stops to collect food.

Males on their hunts needed the surprise factor, so they barely make noises that could ward off prey. On the contrary, female sapiens needed to communicate constantly, permanently, continuously, so they invented speech, spoken language.

Women established the first moral rules to organize access to the new female sex toy or sexual commodity, for this came as a gift the invention of female sensuality, unlike folklore about the club and male rape, now women have become a sexual commodity and needed to value access to it with rules that allowed and prohibited sex between relatives, between men, between women and with children.

Morals, tradition, Ethics were invented, so religion was the next step.

The woman lived in a privileged situation in the pre-technological era, when work meant breaking stones with a sledgehammer, not as it is now, when working behind a computer keyboard or in a truck with automatic transmission and power steering that even a quadriplegic can drive.

The woman invented chauvinism so that the male didn't even suspect that he was the slave of work: hunting, killing, doing everything for the family in exchange for glory, otherwise, he wouldn't deserve the title of strong, brave, powerful male.

 , in his **'Discourse on the Origin of Human Inequalities'** , makes an essay on the process of formation of the liberal State, referring to the value of private property and the social contract that founded the liberal State.

The milestone in the creation of society and the liberal State, for Rousseau, was when the differentiation of social classes emerged, which was the moment when the female sapiens began to be a farmer, began to accumulate, or save for future use, the collection product and agriculture, forming a first heritage.

From the moment that the human couple of male and female sapiens stopped being nomads, and fenced/delimited a piece of territory for themselves and said "this is mine" then there arose, at that moment, the liberal society, the State arose liberal founded on the recognition of private property by an authority created to care for the right to property.

According to Rousseau, the sociability of man is not a natural ability or characteristic; the state of nature is characterized by the sufficiency of wild instinct, in contrast to the state of society which is characterized by the sufficiency of Enlightenment, positivist reason, above instinct.

The natural man is amoral, does not understand vices or virtues, does not need society or the State.

The principle of society, and vices, arose with the possession of goods, that is, when the first private property was declared, when the differentiation between rich and poor, between owners and non-owners arose.

There has never been such a female genocide in human history as Maria da Penha and all militant feminists try to prove.

There was the Nazi genocide against Jews. Christian and Muslim genocide in the Crusades and Inquisitions.

Genocide of peoples at war, genocide of indigenous peoples, genocide of blacks, genocide of Bosnians in Srebrenica and Sarajevo by the Serbs, but there has never been a female genocide in human history.

THE ALIBI Sensible women do not blame men for a hypothetical and unlikely situation of sexist oppression. Ask yourself: why only now have women found themselves oppressed by sexism?

Ask yourself if there was any fact in the history of humanity that proves that machismo existed? Claiming heavy redress against sexist pseudo-discrimination is more absurd than claiming redress for Africa's kidnapped former black slaves. Who would perform such nonsense! How many historical errors will ever be compensated for?

The Hundred Years War?

The Discovery of Brazil and the Indigenous Massacre?

Don Manuel's Napoleonic invasion of Portugal?

South Africa's apartheid?

the Spanish swindle of the gold of the Maya, Inca and Aztec that lasted 300 years of plunder and the massacre of these peoples?

But, women created the myth of chauvinism and are earning legal compensation for something that has never been proven nor demonstrated with facts and evidence: the myth of the female negative distinction.

Males are extremely violent, die murdered at a rate ten times greater than women are murdered, blacks at a rate twenty-two times greater than women, gay men are murdered at a rate, - in proportion to the number of gays - 660 times bigger! The male is being blamed for his evolutionary success over the past 150 years, as in previous years and centuries being male was an unbearable burden given the advantages of being a woman.

Until two hundred years ago the survival of the human species was divided between the role of the human male and the role of the human female. The female took care of the offspring and domestic sustenance and the male hunted, fought, worked with the tools he created himself. The work was so painful that humanity was constantly enslaving more disorganized peoples and less well-off civilizations to exploit the few available sources of energy.

After many millennia of cutting trees, breaking stones, dragging and piling masses, the male invented machines to help him work with less physical and mental effort. It was only with the discovery by the male of electricity, the wheel, the screw, the inclined plane, the lever, the pulley, the axe, Geometry, Chemistry that it was possible to substitute slave labor for the work of machines.

So the England that made the Industrial Revolution and for commercial interests was the first to fight human slavery to spread its steam engines around the world. Where has woman been all this time, when wars were eye-to-eye, thrusting sword and spear into the enemy's belly and carrying the world on the backs and backs of animals?

I answer: being exploited by chauvinism, at home,
taking care of children and feeding while the
oppressive male carried the world with tears, sweat
and blood. Human work has changed a lot
today. There is no dependence on human brute force,
machines do almost everything.

This is the world feminists claim. A little world without
physical work, without sacrifice and without
sweating. To justify their sluggishness and complete
historical alienation, indifference, inability to painful
and hard work in the history of civilization, the woman
is now blame the male for not having participated in
this process progress.

The woman was for millions of years privileged,
being spared from all the arduous and dangerous
work, she was protected and supported by the heavy
male work. Until today, women still flee from heavy
work and hard and dangerous areas (Formula 1,
motocross, Electrical Engineering, Surfing,
Parachuting, Mechanical Engineering, Physics). Now
that human work is carried out and developed behind
a machine or computer, when even a paraplegic can
drive a cart, a ship, an airplane, the woman presents
herself with all the coziness, claiming her equality
condition, ignoring that the male has never been and
will never be your tormentor. We demand apologies
from feminists for this false accusation. The big male.

The male is endangered

It's not what you're thinking.

It's not a war of the sexes.

The male is violent. Too violent.

The male is causing his own extinction.

Typically about 51 female babies are born for every 50 male babies.

In some cities, such as Salvador, Bahia, after eighteen years, of these 51 male babies born, about 40 males are alive, and all 51 females. Ten men died from violence.

In the other Bahian city of Eunápolis, the Brazilian city with the highest rate of youth violence in Brazil, the cold statistic hides another truth: it is black youth who are being decimated. There is no man with university level superior in Eunapolis, Eunápolis the colleges have 100% of enrolled women, there is no man enrolled in any of there top courses.

These are IBGE data.

In Rio de Janeiro, there are 87 males for every 100 women at age eighteen, when about 102 girls are born for every 100 boys.

If real women are concerned about the preservation of the male species, think about it: in the violent mortality statistics, around 29 people die in Brazil for every 100 thousand inhabitants, on average, in the most violent places this number is 39 murders for every one hundred thousand inhabitants (In Maceió there are 91 homicides for every one hundred thousand inhabitants, 90% of them are men), and around 28.6 males are murdered for each group of one hundred thousand inhabitants and around 1.4 women are murdered for each group of 100,000 inhabitants.

Even more shocking to think that about 2 black men die for every white man murdered in Brazil.

It's racial genocide. Ethnocide .

For every woman murdered eleven white men are murdered and about 22 black men are murdered (0.9 gays will be murdered in the same time frame - **6% of the gay population**)!

If we consider that in Canada 1.9 people are murdered for every 100,000 inhabitants and that in Norway or Denmark 0.9 people are murdered for every 100,000 inhabitants, unfortunately the number of women murdered in Brazil for every 100,000 inhabitants is one a perfectly civilized number for the Canadian standard of deaths in general, and only twice that of Norway or Denmark, with the number of blacks murdered in Brazil being about a hundred times greater!

Who is the biggest victim of violence in Brazil: answer women, before starting a campaign against violence that doesn't come close to genocide. Save the blacks! Save the males! Then save the women, Maria da Penha! Blurred public policies mean a waste of public resources. Public policy should not be the result of responsive spasms, and only public satisfaction of mass hysteria.

Someone in Government should be cool-headed enough to stop in the face of a tragedy and stop acting only responsively and do something in Brazil that has almost never been done since Roberto Campos: planning, obviously followed by studies, your inseparable companion.

Thus, because of these distortions, we saw the emergence of racial quotas, later expanded to social quotas, we saw the emergence of school grant policies, then expanded to family grants. From a hiccup or a half-baked solution to a half-baked solution, we are crawling towards the real answers.

While the murder of women is only 10% of the total number of homicides, the Government does not implement a security policy for the rest of the murders of men, which are only 90% of the total, it prefers to respond to feminist hysteria with the Maria da Penha Law of the male genocide of 90% of males, with the greatest crime of all being the extermination of blacks who are murdered in 90% more numbers than whites.

This is public security policy, and not this misleading, distorted, false, prejudiced, slanderous, manipulative and lying propaganda. Therefore, inequality is almost nil in the wild state of nature (pre- socialized stage) of man, the inequalities resulted from society, from social interactions; when one talks about society, one talks about inequality, one talks about poverty and wealth, according to Rousseau.

"Repeat a lie many times and it turns out to be a great truth," says Goebels, Hitler's propaganda minister! Exceptional laws in Brazil distort the ethnic-sexual-age-geographic stratification Blurred public policies mean a waste of public resources. Public policy should not be the result of responsive spasms, and only public satisfaction of mass hysteria.

This would be public security policy, and not this false, distorted, false, prejudiced, slanderous, manipulative and lying propaganda. The federal government on March 13, 2013 launched a program to eliminate violence against women at a cost of R$265 million for a period of two years to build houses in all Brazilian capitals at an average unit cost of R$4 .3 million to "Casas da Mulher Brasileira" with zero tolerance.

Based on data that there were around 70,200 cases of violence against women in Brazil in the previous year, which gives the statistical indicator of 0.368 cases of violence for every 100,000 inhabitants.

The difference to between this number and the indicator of violence in Maceió who was 91 murders (not just violence) general per hundred thousand inhabitants better explains what you can do to hysteria in public policy unreasonable and disproportionate! Obviously, this index (0.3689 per

100,000 inhabitants) will hardly be lowered, as it is below the violence index of countries like Denmark, Sweden and Finland!

I - How much does a good wife cost?

What would be the price of a wife like Michelle Obama, wife of the President of the United States of North America, Barak Obama, or, the monetary value of a wife like Hillary Clinton, wife of former US President Bill Clinton?

If they could go back in time, certainly the regret of having married wives who left enormous material, financial and emotional losses, in other cases, bankruptcies, and ultimately death or paths that led to death indirectly, why these disastrous companions crossed in their lives as an accident, to their unlucky husbands and partners.

What would the former mayor of São Paulo, Celso Pita, do if he could go back in time to the date of his marriage to his ex-wife Nilcéia Pita; they would do the same if they knew before what happened later, certainly they would not also marry Dudu Nobre with Adriana Bom-Bom, Seal with Heidi Klum or Romário.

The id and main was in this study is not to evaluate the

sentimental or psychosocial aspect of marriage, but try to estimate the economic and financial value of an effective wife, effective and efficient through the wedding risk analysis in an objective way to answer to the question: how much is a wife worth?

When analyzing the huge patrimonial, professional or political damage caused by a risk partner, which otherwise should provide cooperation and collaboration, it brings bad luck, so let's compare and identify the candidates for wives who produce a potential of qualities to arrive up to a financially estimated quote from a valuable partner.

So, a wife like Michelle Obama, or Hillary Clinton, or like Mrs Bill Gates, or like Mrs Barbara Bush. How much would each of these precious wives be worth? Certainly these gems are worth a few tens and even hundreds of Millions of US Dollars, (Tens of billions in the case of Mrs Bill Gates).

What are the parameters for evaluating the pricing requirements of an efficient wife? What is the monetary value of a gem identified as a valuable partnership is what will be dealt with from now on.

II – First Part
The Risk Analysis

The risk analysis method will be used here considering the list of risk factors in a candidate through the collected objective answers to establish a valuable spouse according to the score based on the objective risk factors questionnaire. This score will be weighted by another control question quiz based on the risk quiz.

IV - Conclusions:

The Valley A Good Wife

a good wife will yield many years of a good marriage or a stable relationship providing:

a) emotional support;

b) Material support;

c) Financial support;

d) Impulse in the career;

e) Heritage progress;

f) Peace and tranquility .

How to Price a Wife?

If the result of the risk assessment questionnaires is positive with low or no risk, what should be done is to add up the assets and income of the couple accumulated throughout the
relationship, annualizing the monthly income.

After "x" years, the calculated amount represents the couple's equity; thus, the value of the wife is the value equal to at least 50% of the calculated amount.

An excellent low-income wife or partner can represent a price of at least US $240,000 over ten years;

An excellent middle-class spouse or partner can represent a price of at least US $600,000 over ten years.

An excellent wife or partner of high economic class can represent, over ten years, a price of at least US $ 2,400 thousand!

A wife like Michelle Obama goes on ten years of living with her famous husband Barak Obama over US $ 10 million Americans !

Annual income reference table

Economic classes Annual income in R$ thousand

Low 24

Medium 60

High 240

V – Clumsy Wives

This increasingly common behavior deserves a separate theory.

Don't be discouraged when looking for a good wife. It's just that no one told you that today this is strenuous and not very fruitful work. They, the good wives, and the good women, are in extinction.

Precisely at the inflection moment of civilization when practically all human physical work could be totally replaced by computerized machines, by robots, for example, industries without a single soul have already existed for more than two decades, such as a train-train manufacture. plane landing in Australia, without a single human presence and remotely controlled from Boeing's control center in Seattle, USA.

Other examples: the interplanetary
spacecraft Curiosity landed on the ground of the Solar
Planet Mars automatically, because the radio signals
that could control it would not reach there on Mars in
time to monitor and control the landing, monitor the
approach and landing maneuvers by that these signals
traveling at the speed of light would reach
the spacecraft with a delay of more than sixteen
minutes!

Even human intellectual work is in
crisis. Computerized programming code generator
systems replace and in some cases surpass human
intellectual and physical capacity, such as systems
called "case" that design, write, document, analyze
and deploy entire computerized networked information
systems encoded in PHP, Oracle , Java, Javascript,
better than any system analysts or human computer
programmers could ever do!

Computer Aided Design CAD systems design
engineering projects with a perfection that surpasses
the most skilled human designer.

What does it mean?

It means that after more than eight thousand years of total absence of the female gender during the scientific and technological achievements of human civilization, when the male gender was in the forefront creating all sciences and 99.9999% of patents and art objects, and poetry, inventions and scientific and historical discoveries, works of art, then faced with the total absence of the other genre, which watched everything passively, now comes, at the height of humanity's hegemony before the advent of intelligent machines, to dispute the spoils of humanity's decay, translated into the conquest that is summarized in exchanging the role of housewife for occupation outside the home.

Is this the greatest achievement of women? Exchange the narrow perspective of home life for the narrow perspective of life subordinate to the slave system disguised as wage labor for most of these new workers?

This will be the four-hundredth time I read a feminist manifesto and reproduce this excerpt without even achieving an accurate rebuttal! Here it goes:

"I would be glad to agree that the woman got there! I love rooting for the oppressed, even out of mechanical solidarity, because I'm black and I know what it is.

The politically innocent created a false climate that the woman finally got there! I wish it were true! We blacks and women have a long way to go to prove our competence in front of the western white man.

Men created practically everything that exists in modern life without allowing the slightest female participation, as they created, among other things: submarine; Steamship, Aircraft Vehicles, Computer Operating Systems digitized and analog to computerized, propeller helicopters, devices Electric, generators Electric, Welding, Ball Pen, Washer, Hair dryers, Plate eletric of ceramic, semiconductor, Microprocessors: invented, discovered the Physics, Chemistry, Mathematics, Geography, Philosophy, Psychology, Medical, Anthropology, Sociology, Astronautics, Astrology, Engineering and finally, left almost nothing for women to discover or invent. This fact has left women in such a situation that they are unable to prove their intellectual qualities due to the total absence of any opportunity left by males.

There is no historical fact supporting the theory that men have historically oppressed women by leaving them in this state of total submission and unimportance that required an international liberation and liberalization movement. It would be a transnational and intertemporal sexist conspiracy at a time when the continents did not even imagine the existence of each other, in the eras of pre- colonization (pre-Columbian) and pre- discoveries of the Indies, Americas and Africa; how much daydream...!

In order to reach the best positions in the job market that really count and are worthwhile in this change of occupation, women would need to be their own boss, or be their own boss. In the first case, it would need financial capital; in the second case it would need intellectual capital. In both cases, I would need to choose between motherhood and professional activity outside the home.

Thus, motherhood would be postponed or excluded, or supplied by another woman: the domestic nanny.

With so many setbacks in the path of their success in the world of work outside the home, the female gender, in addition to discovering the wildness of competition in the labor market, still has to face, as a minority segment, all the prejudices and minimizing expectations of the professional market about its capacity not yet fully tested and proven in areas where it is absent, such as in car and motorcycle competitions, in engineering areas, finally in areas considered "hard" of human activity, as it has always done throughout history, when the male of the genre broke rocks and waged wars with the sledgehammer and sword, before the inventions of the jackhammer and guided missile, computerized, stealthy and intelligent.

So there is an undeclared war between the
genders. The privilege market is a zero-sum
market. For a new member to be admitted to the elite,
someone will have to give up their place at the top to
the intruding intruder. And that empty place is the
male's.

Each new vacancy filled in the higher courts by a
woman represents one less male in the law courts.

Novice theories suggest, with scientific support,
proclaim the intellectual or emotional superiority of the
female gender.

They just didn't explain why the human female had to
wait millions of years to demonstrate her superiority,
which in itself would deserve a serious psychiatric,
psychological or psychoanalytic evaluation!

But the victimization of the female segment has been
politically successful in the ideological construction
of androphobic feminism in the Western world, in favor
of women, on the male's sense of guilt, for millennia of

oppression of women.

The Maria da Penha Law criminalized male behavior and turned the exception procedure into a rule, transforming the preventive removal of the home partner into an home in fact divorce, an extreme unconditional, radical, draconian banning of their movable property even before the formalization of the process of separation and overriding any pre-existing agreement to the union, violating the constitutional principles of due process of law, of ample defense, of the presumption of innocence.

This is a massive victory for feminism!

The male is violent.

The greatest and the only agent in the history of humanity is the dominator, adventurer, entrepreneur, trailblazer, the male, who is also the protagonist of the greatest violence against all of humanity.

Why is only the female exceptionally protected from male aggression?

The same intensity and radicality of this protection provided by Maria da Penha is not intended to protect and extend the prevention of male violence against another male, or against the child, or against the elderly, or against the disabled.

Because?

This fact would explain the success of feminist militancy in its project of siege and surrender of the male and its reduction to the supporting role, previously destined and occupied by the female of the species.

Given these facts, choosing the wrong wife can bring home the worst enemy, the worst nightmare!

We are at war, and in a war it is good strategy to know and study the enemy's strategic plans and tactical movements, to know their arsenal and military objectives.

The goal of feminism is the total submission of the male, whose project is at a very advanced stage in countries such as: Finland, Norway, Sweden, Denmark, Iceland and Canada; encounters strong resistance in: Russia, Germany, Brazil, USAN; is incipient in: Spain, Portugal, Italy, African continents, Asia and the Middle East.

A verification of the humiliating condition of the male in the Nordic countries is a good indication of where this strategy would go: the end of the family, the decrease in fertility, consequently, the decrease in the human population, low scientific productivity. It would be a risk to the survival of the human species!

In exchange for a sexual crumb, mitigated affection and lack of attention for a high fixed cost, and unlimited variable cost, such are marriages in 90% of cases, which have turned into a civilized form of "sexual embezzlement", which forces the male to accept financing for the physical decay of his former muse, now aged, flaccid, fallen, complaining more and more about almost everything, jealous, possessive, castrating and vigilant of his patrimony, waiting for the first occasion to propose a fat divorce agreement paid handsomely for the rest of his asexual and idle life. This is the plan of 80% of androphobic feminist wives .

Feminism is the offspring of the unconfessed androphobia of women who seek a historical repair of gender inequality that is supposed to be solely the male's fault.

The Feminine Reality

The reality as it presents itself to the female mind's cognition is reduced to a desire to see the representation of facts and objects as a synthesis between the subjective and the objective.

No matter how visible and real this world is, its existence depends solely on the awareness of its existence in the mind and eyes of the one who sees it, in this case, in the female mind the representation of reality is detached and displaced in its world where the thing- itself does not represent itself without the necessary interpretation and is guided by the will to represent reality that is the vital force in women.

In this way appearances have an unsurpassed iconographic force.

When a woman wears a four-inch high-heeled shoe, in her representation of reality she is actually ten centimeters taller, but for the male perspective of reality she is still the same height, the heel is just an artifice; not for the woman, who in fact is actually taller now. This is how it happens when using makeup, all that painted beauty is incorporated into her feminine appearance, as she sees herself in the mirror from the perspective of the reality of the female gaze, but for the male, that cosmetic beauty is just a bit of paint about that old familiar face: it's not part of her beauty, she's just a painted character overlapping the known reality.

That's why women dress and paint themselves for other women, not men, for the masculine gaze does not add the modified version of feminine appearance to its catalog of universal object recognition. All that makeup, the high heels, the elongated and dyed hair, are additions to her persistent memory object that does not change in her identification of the primitive perception of the updated and revised original model.

This difference in the perception of reality between men and women defines the entire philosophy that separates the two worlds.

The only world that exists for each individual is only the individual's perception of the world, so men and women live permanently isolated in their perceptions of the world, immersed in their subjectivities, objectified in their own translations of what would be their realities, in any hypotheses these worlds never communicate, never meet.

What is the natural object for a woman if not her desire
to see represented or representing in it her idealized
vision of the object!

Entering this world of female representation consists in
understanding the forms of description of these objects
by their external forms belonging to their catalog of
universal objects that make up their library, or their
dictionary, which is their manual for the representation
of reality.

This female dictionary is composed of:
    a) aesthetics,
    b) feeling,
    c) emotion,
    d) dreams,
    e) wishes,
    f) sensations,
    g) images,
    h) senses,
    i) colors,
    j) textures,
    k) smells,
    l) flavors,
    m) lights and
    n) shadows,

o) sounds,
p) gestures,
q) adjectives,
r) symbolisms,
s) protocols,
t) rhythms,
u) moments, carefully chosen

because every object and female acts have intentionality, rather than objective results or causality, and obviously do without subsequent consequences, justifications or explanations but merely the impression they make, rather than rational and deterministic results.

What matters most is the emotion and the effect on the senses they cause. Trying to get an explanation for female acts and behaviors is like trying to explain a work of art: it would remove or nullify all the emotion and objectification that the artist intended to give in his work.

The man's gaze is like the gaze of the gardener who continues to seek to provide his garden with the means to support life, watering, fertilizing, pruning and maintaining the proportions between the plants geometrically: the female gaze is the rose itself in this garden, that rose that even without being aware of itself as a rose, but accepting the care of the gardener, whose objectification is the survival of plants, but even if he does not admire the beauty and aesthetics of his garden, this does not prevent him from knowing what the plants under your care need to reign with their beauties.

Although the goals are independent, gardener and roses are interdependent, regardless of awareness or not of this reality.

The existence of the rose guarantees the employment of the gardener; the existence of the gardener guarantees the survival and splendor of the rose. One does not even need to like or love the other, so they go together united by the function of mutual dependence and the subjective utilities of that mutual dependence.

That should be the essence of a marriage.

The woman invented the family, moral love, beauty, monogamy, jealousy, to maintain the exclusivity and fidelity of the male through affection.

The feminine world

How complicated it is for a man to understand the feminine world!

Not so much.

The masculine world, or the world according to the masculinized view, cannot be interpreted. The world according to the male's cognitive perspective is a fragmented world, compartmentalized and heuristically reconstructed according to predictable rules, principles, laws, concepts, doctrines, norms and expectations of behavior (institutions).

The world as it appears to the female gaze is constantly reinterpreted according to impressions that fit expectations and subjective sensory perceptions within the concreteness established by the lived, intuitive, sensory experience and the memory of facts.

How are facts seen from this female perspective? It is the facts of perception that harmonize with reality.

The woman deals with the perception of facts, eliminating the barrier and the limit of separation between the subject and the object.

It is opposite to the masculine, analyzing reality from an individual point of view. Everything that presents itself to female perception occurs as an intentional purposeful emotional object. The objective of the perception of facts for the female is to reach the intention of the essences of attitudes, decisions and behaviors. It seeks to interpret the world through the awareness of a particular female subject, according to their experiences.

Believes in instantly capturing phenomena in a sensitive, emotional and sensory way, considers that all consciousness is "awareness of some substance", but consciousness is not considered a substance, but formed by acts of perception, imagination, passion, emotions and other acts internals of female beings.

It is based on the search for the motivational essence of a given phenomenon through the sensory reduction process; all things are characterized by being unfinished in a constant process of modification.

The woman elaborates a method of observation of facts, scientifically, regarding the description and classification of events in search of a previous recognition, on new facts, which always fall within the scope of some lived experience prior to the memory of the present facts, performing a anamnesis to recognize and clarify the phenomenon under observation that considers the vision of the particular female spectator subject.

Plato solves this problem with his Theory of Ideas. What is permanent in an object is the Idea; more precisely, the participation of this object in its corresponding Idea. And this object is not an Idea, but an incomplete subjective, personal and sensitive representation of that concrete object.

Note the example of the tree: what makes it to be itself and to be a tree (and not something else), despite its difference from what it was when it was younger in its vegetative development stages, in other stages of its growth and metamorphosis from its seedling or seed stage, and of other trees of other species (and even of trees of the same species) is its singular characteristic participation in the Tree Idea; and its change and variety are due to the fact that it is a pale representation of the General and generic Idea of always being a Tree species.

Plato also elaborated a gnosiological theory, that is, a theory that explains how things can be known, or even a theory of knowledge.

According to him, when seeing an object repeatedly, a person gradually remembers the generic Idea of that object that he saw in the world of Ideas. To explain how this happens, Plato resorts to a myth (or a metaphor) according to which, before birth, each person's soul lived in a star, where the stores of general and generic Ideas are located.

When a person is born, his soul is "thrown" to Earth, and the impact that takes place makes him forget what he saw in the star. But seeing an object appear in different shapes (like the different trees you can see), the soul remembers the generic Idea of that object that was seen in the star. Such a memory, in Plato, is called anamnesis .

Reminiscence One of the conditions for inquiring or investigating about Ideas is that we are not in a state of complete ignorance about them. Otherwise, we would have neither the desire nor the power to seek them out. In view of this, it is a necessary condition, for such investigation, that we have in our soul some kind of knowledge or memory of our contact with Ideas (this contact occurred before our own birth) and that we remember the Ideas when seeing them reproduced pale in things. In this way, the whole of Platonic science is a reminiscence.

The investigation of Ideas presupposes that souls preexisted in a divine region where they contemplated Ideas. We can take as an example the Myth of the Winged Pair, located in Plato's Phaedrus dialogue. In this dialogue, Plato compares the human race to winged cars. Everything we do good, gives strength to our wings. Everything we do wrong, takes strength from our wings. Over time we did so many wrong things that our wings lost strength and, without them to sustain us, we fell into the Sensitive World, where we live until today. From this moment on, we were condemned to see only the shadows of the World of Ideas (see Plato's The Myth of the Cave).

So the female worldview is that everything we can know of the world comes down to these phenomena, these ideal objects that exist in the mind, each designated by a word that represents its essence, its "meaning." The objects of life are concrete data apprehended in pure intuition, with the purpose of discovering essential structures of the acts (noesis) and the objective entities that correspond to them (noema).

For women, everything that is informed by the senses is changed into an experience of consciousness, an event that consists of being aware of something. Things, images, fantasies, acts, relationships, thoughts, events, memories, feelings, etc. they constitute experiences of consciousness.

For women, the study of our experiences, our states of consciousness, the ideal objects of this event, which is to be aware of something, form their encyclopedia (repository) for recognizing reality; we shouldn't worry about whether or not it corresponds to objects in the world outside our mind. The interest for the female perceptual consciousness is not the world that exists, but the way in which knowledge of the world is realized for her.

The reduction of experienced and observed facts requires the suspension of attitudes, epoché, beliefs, theories, and suspending the knowledge of things in the external world in order to focus the woman exclusively on the experience in focus, because this is the reality for Is it over there.

When a woman puts on high heels, she becomes really tall; when a woman receives a rose, the rose does not represent love: it is love itself, so she keeps it lovingly forever if she can keep love; when a woman dyes her hair blonde she is really blonde; when a woman puts on makeup she is not a painting, she is her image three times more beautiful.

The woman does not play with symbols, she is the symbol itself. A man sees a painted woman, a woman sees herself in nature, dazzling through the painting of her face. There is a huge difference in the world as a representation of reality between man and woman.

The Noesis is the act of perceiving and Noema is the perception of the object - these are the two poles of experience.

The thing as a fact of consciousness (noema) is the thing that matters, and refers to the call to "things in themselves." "Reduction of sensible experience" therefore means restricting knowledge to the state of experience of consciousness, disregarding the real world, putting it "in parentheses", which is not to say that one should doubt the existence of the world like the radical idealists Skeptics and positivists doubt, but worry about knowledge of the world in the way it takes place in the perspective of the phenomenon and in the view of the world that women have.

Experience (Erlebnis) is the whole mental act; it has to encompass the objects of the experiences, because the experiences are intentional and in them the reference to a previously experienced memory fact is essential.

Consciousness is characterized by intentionality, because it is always the awareness of something familiar. This intentionality is the essence of consciousness that is represented by meaning, the name by which consciousness refers to each fact.

In "The Psychology of a point of view of experience" - 1874 - Franz Brentano says, "We can thus define the mind events saying that they are those who, precisely because they are intentional, contain themselves in them a fact." This is tantamount to state , like Husserl, that mental events are independent of the existence of their exact replica in the real world because they contain the event itself.

The description of mental acts thus involves the description of their meanings, but only as experiences and without assuming or asserting their existence in the concrete world. The event need not actually exist.

It was a new use of the term "intentionality" that previously applied only to the element of the concrete fact's will to exist.

What matters is not whether the thing exists or not or how it exists in the world, but the way in which knowledge of the world happens as intuition, the act by which the woman immediately apprehends the knowledge of something she comes across - which is also an act primarily given on which all else is to be founded in terms of a return to intuition, Anschauung, is the perception of essence.

Furthermore, the emphasis on intuition needs to be understood as a refutation of any merely speculative approach to philosophy.

Its approach is "concrete", dealing with the way of seeing the various types of consciousness does not restrict its data to the range of sensitive experiences, as it admits non-sensitive data (categories) such as value relations, as long as they are presented intuitively (analytical categories).

The function of words for a woman is not to name everything we see or hear, but to highlight the recurring patterns in her experience as a woman. They identify current sense data as being in the same group as others they have recorded before.

A word does not describe a single experience, but a group or type of experience; the word "table" describes all the various sense-data which one normally consults regarding the appearances or sensations of "table". Thus, everything a woman thinks, wants, loves or fears is intentional, that is, it refers to one of these universals (which are meanings and, as such, are events and facts of consciousness). And in turn, the set of events, the set of meanings, has a greater meaning, which encompasses all the others, that is what the word "Universal" means.

John Locke The largest of the empiricist philosophers searched
his Essay Concerning Human Understanding (1690) demonstrate that all ideas are records of sense impressions (or are derived from combinations of associations between these id and ias sensitive origin), and criticized the thought Descartes (1596-1650) that there would be some
id and were going to be innate - that man would have in

mind at birth - such as, for example, the id and was perfection.

According to John Locke, something is sent by objects and is captured by our senses and give cause to the formation of the id and ias. This thought is the basis of the corpuscular theory of light.

David Hume Even more forcefully than his predecessor Locke, he denied the value of logical reasoning and denounced that the relation of cause and effect is not sufficient as truth, since we find nothing between cause and effect but that one accident usually follows another. We are used to calling the first accident a cause just because it always happens before the second we call an effect (spatial-temporal correlation).

Immanuel Kant According to the philosophy of knowledge (Criticism) of Immanuel Kant (1724-1804), we cannot fully know things, because not all the signs we receive from things are accepted by the mind, and it follows that we cannot fully know the real.

We know of the real only what the mind can assimilate, and what he called phenomenon; what remains unknowable to us he called the noumeno.

So Kant took the series of concepts that Aristotle had listed as what we can say about things, and turned it into a series of categories that are what we can know about things.

For Kant the real, concrete datum has validity, but never absolute or apodictic validity. Husserl equally doubts the scientific knowledge of facts and, for him, what must be sought is the scientific knowledge of essences.

The woman must be considered in the male gaze in view of the fact represented that in her feminine mind the impression caused by the objects and facts correspond to her own reality, no matter what the external situation, and because this feminine construction differs from the common pattern of ideal objects in the male mind with respect to the same sense stimuli perceived by the female mind.

Male thinking needs to find meaning in the objects of the ideal female world in order to be able to deal with its female mental situation.

The difficulty between the masculine world and the feminine world that arises is the possibility for the masculine to live with his own vision of the world, of his situation and of himself in relation to women.

As subjectivity must also be in the male worldview mode, it is impossible for the male mind to have an intuition of these aspects that is entirely free of its own self, its own thinking, so as to avoid intruding into its perception of the world. certain masculine personal impressions that you would need to avoid.

The male being must seek to understand with his subjectivity the female subjectivity. In fact, it needs a group of consulting psychologists so that their views can add up to a deeper understanding of a phenomenon of " intersubjectivity ".

However, you must remember that, strictly speaking, the male being has no absolutely reliable standard to approve or disapprove of any female behavior, despite being comfortable with the statistics of the normality of female attitudes and customs of what could be called of normal behavior. It will only reduce violence against women when, instead of punishment, sentimental education is taught to men and women. Whoever is willing to die is not afraid to kill.

The desperate and broken heart does not recoil from the threat of punishment. The Taliban that say: Do not be punished by death suicide-pervasive.

None of this will put a stop to violence against women if it is not accompanied by training and conditioning of the sentimental behavior of both men and women, as they will continue to be victims of mistreated love, of the evil of disillusioned love.

When a man kills his love, he is trying to kill the evil that exists within the love relationship, throwing the water out of the bathtub with the baby along.

To live love, it is necessary to learn to love and the State needs to teach how the couple should deal with their feelings. Punishment is not a solution, nor is the remedy and consolation for hearts and bodies torn by the pain and wounds of hopeless love.

Blacks in the country die almost twice as often as whites. Between 2002 and 2008, the number of homicides of white victims fell in the country, while the number of black victims rose.

According to the study, in 2002, 45.8% more blacks died than whites, in 2005 this number rose to 67.1% and, in 2008, it reached the peak of 103.4%, which means that for every white dead, two blacks die.

The difference in homicides between blacks and whites is greater in the Northeast region - where the proportion is one white for every ten black victims of homicide - and smaller in the South region, where the number and proportion is inverted, not in the same intensity, but in the of one black dead for every four white dead.

This difference between the two regions is not surprising, as in the Northeast there are more blacks than whites and in the South the population is mostly white. Double the number of black deaths in relation to whites in Brazil is a fact that confirms what the Black Movement has been denouncing for a long time: there is a genocide of the black population in the country. - It doesn't mean that those die for being black, necessarily. It also reveals that specific public policies are needed for this population, which promote equal opportunities and access to rights.

 IPEA former President Marcelo Nery presents the balance of the disarmament law after ten years:

a) Sales dropped from 57 thousand to 37 thousand firearms;

b) homicides fell by 5.9%; It is not necessary to do a statistical multiple linear regression or to use sophisticated calculations to discover the stupidity of this Law.

They removed about 35% of the new weapons, and collected thousands of weapons that were in the houses of decent people. Bandits don't buy guns in stores, that's been proven. Bandits do not stock up on weapons from decent people, this has been proven. The bandits were not intimidated by the penalties of illegal possession of weapons, this was proven. Crime has decreased (ALMOST NOTHING) disproportionately to the government's effort to combat homicide. But some scoundrel will argue that the population has increased and that without the disarmament and control laws it could have been worse. It turns out that it is not known if it would be worse or not because I am not a psychic, I only know these numbers. Thank you Government for this law that leaves us helpless in the face of criminals who are always sure that in the house of an honest citizen there will never be a firearm waiting for them. PS.: The USA has 50% more inhabitants than Brazil, everyone has guns there, more than 300 million guns for a population of 300 million inhabitants, have a tenth of homicides in Brazil. Thank you internet pacifists, and pajama revolutionaries!

Creates a parallel state, law, special only for the same woman before all the legal defense to maria disposal of rock and even with the conviction of the defendant sought Mrs. Maria da Penha serve tireless militants of always minorities to looking for an alibi , one more , to attack society without stopping , to create
the objective conditions to implant a communist state, but , fortunately , it only causes more irritation and commotion due to the always unbalanced and disastrous consequences that aggravate much more than they solve. We entered the era of intolerance, of the only-thought, of the politically correct ideological patrol, of prejudice of prejudice, of boring people of all kinds, ecoboring, homoboring, politicboring, paidob oring. Revolutionaries without a cause. There is no more sexual revolution to be made, no more political turns, nothing to conquer or explore, the era of important causes for humanity is over, only late revolutionaries are left!

Rosanne D'Agostino From G1 in São Paulo

566 comments

The Maria da Penha Law, which entered into force in 2006 to combat violence against women, had no impact on the number of deaths from this type of aggression, according to the study "Violence against women: femicide in Brazil", released on Wednesday Thursday (24) by the Institute of Applied Economic Research (Ipea).